National 5: RMPS Judaism

Stewart's Melville College

ISBN: 9798850026813
Imprint: Independently published

"More than wealth and power, education is the key to human dignity."

-Rabbi Jonathan Saks

CONTENTS

1 NATURE OF GOD

'Hear O Israel, the Lord is our God, the Lord is One.'
(Deuteronomy 6:4)

According to Jewish law, a Jew is any person who is born to a Jewish mother, irrespective of the mother's marital status; or any person who has gone through the formal process of conversion to Judaism. Jewish people live in different continents of the world, speak different languages and hold different views about the ways in which Judaism should be observed. However, those who are committed to Judaism in some form share the **belief in one God**. This belief affects the way Jews interact in the world as everything one sees, hears or experiences is a meaningful encounter with God. Judaism is thus **monotheistic** like other religions such as Christianity and Islam, which came later.

The fundamental belief in one God is declared twice every day in the **Shema** which Jews recite every morning and evening. It's opening sentence states *'Hear O Israel, the Lord is our God, the Lord is One.'* This pronounces the belief in one God to all Jews, who are referred to as the children of Israel.

Jews believe that God is very different from human beings. **He is not a physical entity.** God is infinitely above and beyond everything else that exists (transcendent) or can be imagined. But although He may be far away in the heavens, yet He is also near to listen to prayers.

We can learn much more about God, through the studying the Jewish holy book – known as the Tanakh.

The word Tanakh comes from the first letters of the three different parts of the book:

- **The Torah (T)** which is the first five books of the Hebrew Bible. The Christian Bible also begins with these books, in the part which Christians call the Old Testament.
- **The Nevi'im (N)** which are the books of the Jewish prophets such as Joshua and Isaiah.
- **Ketuvim (K)** which is a collection other important writings.

Jewish people believe that God is the creator of the universe and everything in it. They know this from reading the book of Genesis which gives an account of how God made the world in six days and rested on the seventh.

But the book of Genesis has other stories about God that also help us to find out what he's like – like the story of Sodom and Gomorrah:

In this story, it is told that three angels visited Abraham (the founder of Judaism) but came disguised as men, travellers along the road. Two of them went down to Sodom and Gomorrah, to observe first-hand the wickedness in those cities. The other visitor stayed behind and revealed to Abraham that God was going to destroy the cities because of the evil ways of their people. Abraham began to bargain with God to spare the cities if there were righteous people in them. But when the two angels arrived at Sodom that evening, Abraham's nephew Lot met them at the city gate. Lot and his family lived in Sodom. He took the two men to his home and fed them.

Then all the men of the city surrounded Lot's house and said, "Where are the men who came to you tonight? Bring them out to us so that we can have sex with them." By ancient custom, the visitors were under Lot's protection. But Lot was so infected by the wickedness of Sodom that he offered the men his two virgin daughters instead. Furious, the mob rushed up to break down the door. Thankfully the angels struck the rioters blind. Leading Lot, his wife, and two daughters by the hand they hurried them out of the city.

Lot and his family fled whilst God rained down burning sulphur on Sodom and Gomorrah, destroying the buildings and all the people. Lot's wife disobeyed the angels, looked back, and turned into a pillar of salt.

In short, this story teaches that **God is a Judge** and will punish those who disobey him.

However, it's important to note that **God is also willing to forgive**. Which can be illustrated through the story of David and Bathsheba, found in the book of 2 Samuel.

That tells the story of how one night, King David couldn't sleep so he goes for a walk on the roof. He sees a beautiful woman bathing in the next house. He asks someone who she is and is told, "She's Bathsheba, married to Uriah, one of your elite fighting men). He sends for her and has sex with her, knowing it's wrong. She finds out she's pregnant so David sends for Bathsheba's husband to come home to try to cover up his sin. He talks to Uriah about the battle and sends him home so he'll sleep with his wife and the affair will be hidden.

But Uriah is a man of integrity (he doesn't want to enjoy anything his fellow-soldiers can't enjoy), so he sleeps outside the palace. David tries again the next night, this time getting Uriah drunk. But Uriah still won't go home. Eventually, David sends Uriah back to the front with a note for Joab, the General, to put Uriah in an exposed position where he'll be killed—to make sure by pulling the other troops back and leaving him stranded. Joab does it.

David has committed adultery and murder. But David sends for and marries Bathsheba. The baby has been born and at least nine months have passed, but David has not repented (said sorry for his sin). So, God wills the baby to die.

So how does that show forgiveness?! It shows that God punishes believers to bring them back into fellowship and to show the world that He does not excuse or accept sin. But it's what happened next that matters: David repented he said sorry and showed that he would change, and then God forgave him – giving him and Bathsheba a second son – Solomon. Who went on to be one of the greatest Kings of Israel.

Another example of God's faithfulness can be found in the book of Daniel. In this story, King Darius decreed that no one should be praying to God – they should only worship him as king. But Daniel stayed faithful to God, so Darius threw him into a pit of man-eating lions.

Daniel kept praying though, so God sent an angel to keep the lions away from him – until he could be rescued. This story teaches that God isn't just faithful to His people, but that **He will protect them in times of need.**

Another famous story that shows God's power (and vengeance on the sinful) is of course 'Noah's Ark.' In the book of Genesis, we learn of a man who is faithful to God in all that he does. One day, God informed Noah that he was going to send a great flood to cleanse the earth of its wickedness. Noah was instructed to build an ark that would house his family and a pair of every kind of animal.

Noah faithfully followed God's instructions and constructed the ark, which was a massive boat with three decks. As he completed the ark, animals started to arrive in pairs, as God had commanded. Noah, along with his wife, three sons, and their wives, entered the ark along with the animals.

After everyone and everything was safely on board, the rain started to pour, and the floodwaters covered the entire earth. The flood lasted for forty days and nights, while the ark floated on the water's surface. The ark became a refuge for Noah and all the living creatures.

Finally, the rain stopped, and the floodwaters began to recede. Noah sent out a raven and a dove to find dry land, but they returned without any success. Eventually, the dove returned with an olive leaf, indicating that the floodwaters had sufficiently receded. Noah and his family, along with the animals, left the ark and praised God for their survival.

God made a covenant with Noah, promising never to destroy the earth again with a flood. To symbolize this covenant, God placed a rainbow in the sky as a sign of his promise. Noah and his family then began to repopulate the earth and start anew.

Another example of this can be found in the book of Exodus when God split the Red Sea to allow the Hebrews to escape the Egyptians. This also shows that **He is *omnipotent* or 'all powerful'** and able to do the unimaginable.

If you needed a final warning about God's power and attitude towards wrongdoers, then the story of 2 Kings serves a powerful reminder. In this story, we hear about the prophet Elisha who was going about delivering God's message. As Elisha was traveling to Bethel, a group of young boys came out of the city and mocked him, calling him a baldhead. The boys were disrespectful and made fun of the prophet.

In response to their mockery, Elisha cursed the boys in the name of the Lord. Suddenly, two female bears came out of the woods and mauled forty-two of the boys. The bears attacked and killed them as a consequence of their disrespectful behaviour towards God's prophet.

This story serves as a lesson about respecting God's chosen messengers and the consequences that can follow disobedience and disrespect.

Summary: Beliefs about God

- God is one: 'Hear O Israel, the Lord your God is One.'
- God is the creator: the creator of the universe and everything in it. Stated in Genesis.
- God is all powerful: this is shown in Exodus where He splits the Red Sea
- God is all knowing: In the book of Psalms, it states 'He even knows our inner most thoughts.'
- God is loyal: an example of this is when he saved Noah from the flood in Genesis or when he saved the Hebrews from Egypt.
- God is a protector: God protected Daniel in the pit of lions – sending an angel to protect him.
- God is forgiving: an example of this is in David and Bathsheba. God forgave King David for both adultery and murder, when David repented.
- God is a judge: in Genesis Lot's wife disobeyed the angels and looked backed and was turned into a pillar of salt.

2 DUAL NATURE OF HUMANITY

Jews believe that God created the universe out of nothing. By creating the world in this way, Jews believe that God made it exactly the way He wanted – that is, in a way which involved order, harmony and continuity. Creation separated light from darkness, heaven from earth, and produced vegetation, the sun and the moon, fish, birds and other animals. Everything that was created was deliberate and the sequence in which it was created was also deliberate.

The final goal of God's creation is on the sixth day when both man and woman were created. Man is placed at the top of the scale of Creation. The name that God gave man was **Adam** which comes from the Hebrew word *'adamah'* meaning 'the earth' or 'soil'. Adam was created from the earth. The phrase *'Let us make man'* (Genesis 1 v 26) is not included in the previous verses which describe the creation of other forms. This phrase suggests the deliberation, thought and wisdom that went into the creation of man.

Whilst Judaism teaches that man was made in 'God's image' this does not mean to look like Him, but rather, it means that humanity has the ability to create and to freely do so. However, to be made in the image of God is not only a description of our creative powers; it is also a statement of responsibility about the way we treat others. Do we see God in them? Do we recognize that all people are created in this image – not just famous people or the people who can serve us in some way. As Rabbi Arthur Green wrote - "We are created in the image of God, if you will, and we are obliged to return the favour."

Immediately after creating man, God blesses him and entrusts him with sovereignty over the animal creatures. The intimate relationship between God and human beings is implied by the phrase *'And God said unto him'* as this phrase is exclusively used for man. The statement *'that it was good'* which conveys God's approval after each part of Creation was complete is not specifically made after the creation of man. This is because man is not complete and must always try to improve and develop himself and his world. Jews believe that Creation is on-going in that God guides mankind towards the fulfilment of a purpose.

The story of Creation showed that God has given a blueprint for a happy life, but the human desire for independence upsets this existence.

Only after God told man to cultivate, work on the land and look after it, did He give him permission to eat of its fruits. Humanity's most sacred privilege is freedom of will which is one of the basic principles of Judaism. Jews are required to learn what God has taught about what is right and what is wrong; and they are then left to choose between the alternatives. This includes the ability to obey or disobey God, the ability to choose between good and evil. It is clear that humans are morally responsible for their own actions.

This is a very important principle in Judaism. God does not predetermine whether a human is good or bad. The one rule that God made was a test of the use that humans would make of their freedom. This shows that humanity's spiritual life may require the subordination of his desires to the law of God.

Genesis 3 tells of Eve falling into the temptation of the serpent, eating from the tree of knowledge of good and evil and giving Adam one of its fruits. When Adam replies to God's call and says 'I was afraid, because I was naked' (Genesis 3 v 10), he commits another offence by making an excuse for his wrongful behaviour and concealing the truth. Adam continues to throw the **blame** upon everybody but himself. First, he blames Eve, who then blames the serpent (who didn't have a leg to stand on!) and eventually even God is blamed. Some Jewish Rabbis view this is an example of 'one sin leading to another sin', i.e. **the consequence of sin is further evil.**

Yetzer Tov and Yetzer Harah

Judaism believes that everyone has two opposing inclinations, the moral conscience – the **Yetzer Tov** – and the instinct to survive – the **Yetzer Harah**. However, these inclinations are not bad or good in themselves, but they have the potential to do good or to do evil. They are our natural urges or impulses, and without them we could not function.

The Yetzer Tov is our moral conscience. It can be strengthened by education and by constantly living in a moral way. The more we pay heed to it, the easier it becomes. Conversely, it can wither away if we do not learn how we should behave and if all our actions are governed by self-interest alone.

The Yetzer Harah is our instinct for survival, the need for food, ambition, the wish to succeed, the wish to love, be loved and procreate. When controlled, these instincts are acceptable, even laudable; but uncontrolled, they can be evil. We need food to survive, but if we are greedy and take too much then that is not good for our physical health or our moral health. We are taking more than our fair share. Similarly, the wish to succeed is not bad in itself. Without it, no one would invent things, or create beautiful objects, or buy a house, or wish to improve their own and other people's standard of living.

However, if one cheats in order to succeed, or tells lies in order to get a job ahead of someone else then that is bad. In both these examples the good inclination has failed to modify or control the evil inclination and keep it within civilised bounds. In other words, we need ambition in order to get on in the world – but if that ambition is unchecked by our Yetzer Tov (moral conscience), and is allowed to act regardless of other people, then it becomes evil, which is why it is called the Yetzer Harah, the evil inclination. Again, without the desire to make love we would become extinct, so that is legitimate and not bad in itself. However, if our sexual appetite is unchecked and we become sexual predators regardless of the feelings of the other party, then that is bad. The teachings of the Torah are referred to as the antidote to the Yetzer Harah.

The Yetzer Tov can be strengthened in a number of ways: developing a relationship with God, following the mitzvot carefully, praying or worshipping with other Jews, or even chatting with a Rabbi.

Everyone is born with a Yetzer Harah but the Yetzer Tov isn't developed until the point of maturity. This is the age of twelve for girls and the age of thirteen for boys. This event is marked by the Bat Mitzvah or Bar Mitzvah.

Bat Mitzvahs and Bar Mitzvahs

"Bar Mitzvah" literally means **"son of the commandment."** "Bar" is "son" in Aramaic, which used to be the vernacular of the Jewish people. "Mitzvah" is "commandment" in both Hebrew and Aramaic. "Bat" is daughter in Hebrew and Aramaic. Technically, the term refers to the child who is coming of age, and it is strictly correct to refer to someone as "becoming a bar (or bat) mitzvah." However, the term is more commonly used to refer to the coming of age ceremony itself, and you are more likely to hear that someone is "having a bar mitzvah."

Under Jewish Law, children are not obligated to observe the commandments, although they are encouraged to do so as much as possible to learn the obligations they will have as adults. At the age of twelve for girls, and thirteen for boys, children become obligated to observe the commandments. The bar mitzvah ceremony formally marks the assumption of that obligation, along with the corresponding right to take part in leading religious services, to form binding contracts, to testify before religious courts and to marry.

A Jewish boy automatically becomes a bar mitzvah upon reaching the age of 13 years, and a girl upon reaching the age of 12 years. No ceremony is needed to confer these rights and obligations. The popular bar mitzvah ceremony is not required, and does not fulfill any commandment. The bar or bat mitzvah is a relatively modern innovation, not mentioned in the Talmud, and the elaborate ceremonies and receptions that are commonplace today were unheard of as recently as a century ago.

During Shabbat services on a Saturday shortly after the boy's 13th birthday, the celebrant is called up to the Torah to recite a blessing over the weekly reading.

Today, it is common practice for the bar mitzvah celebrant to do much more than just say the blessing. It is most common for the celebrant to learn the entire haftarah portion, including its traditional chant, and recite that. In some congregations, the celebrant reads the entire weekly Torah portion, or leads part of the service, or leads the congregation in certain important prayers. The celebrant is also generally required to make a speech, which traditionally begins with the phrase "today I am a man." The father traditionally recites a blessing thanking God for removing the burden of being responsible for the son's sins (because now the child is old enough to be held responsible for himself).

In modern times, the religious service is followed by a reception that is often as elaborate as a wedding reception. In Orthodox practice, women are not permitted to participate in religious services in these ways, so a bat mitzvah, if celebrated at all, is usually little more than a party. In other movements of Judaism, the girls do exactly the same thing as the boys.

It is important to note that a bar mitzvah is not the goal of a Jewish education, nor is it a graduation ceremony marking the end of a person's Jewish education. Jews are obligated to study Torah throughout our lives. To emphasize this point, some rabbis require a bar mitzvah student to sign an agreement promising to continue Jewish education after the bar mitzvah.

Gifts

Gifts are commonly given after a bar or bat mitzvah ceremony. They are given at the reception, not at the service itself. Please keep in mind that a bar mitzvah is incorporated into an ordinary sabbath service, and many of the people present at the service may not be involved in the bar mitzvah. The nature of the gift varies significantly depending on the community. At one time, the most common gifts were a nice pen set or something useful for school. In many communities today, however, the gifts are the same sort that you would give any child for his 13th birthday.

Summary: Dual Nature of Humanity

- Jews believe that each human being has two sides of their nature.
- Yetzer harah is our survival instinct and Yetzer tov is our moral conscience.
- Yetzer harah is essential for us to function and is not bad.
- Our yetzer harah must be balanced by our yetzer tov otherwise we will likely sin.
- Following the Torah can strengthen the yetzer tov to ensure it balances the yetzer harah.
- Humans have responsibility to do good as they are the only part of creation gifted with a moral conscience by God.
- God created Humans in His own image by moulding them from dust and breathing life into them.
- Yetzer tov is developed at thirteen for a boy and twelve for a girl - marked by the bar/bat mitzvah.

3 FREE WILL

If humans do not have free will – the ability to choose – then actions are morally and religiously insignificant: a murderer who kills because she is compelled to do so would be no different than a righteous person who gives charity because she is compelled to do so.

Jewish tradition assumes that our actions *are* significant. According to the Bible, the Jews were given the Torah and commanded to follow its precepts, with reward and retribution to be meted out accordingly. For Judaism to make sense, then, humans must have free will.

The Free Will Problem

There are theological problems with the idea of human free will. Jewish tradition depicts God as intricately involved in the unfolding of history. The Bible has examples of God announcing predetermined events and interfering with individual choices. Rabbinic literature and medieval philosophy further develop the notion of divine providence: God watches over, guides, and intervenes in human affairs. How can this be reconciled with human free will?

There is also a philosophical problem, which derives from the conception of God as omnipotent and omniscient: If God is all-powerful and all-knowing, then God must know what we will do before we do it. Doesn't this predetermine our choices? Doesn't this negate free will?

Modern science has raised yet another problem. Some contemporary scientific thinking and research attributes much of human behaviour to biological and psychological factors. If these factors in large part, determine our behaviour, how can we be held responsible for our actions?

Some people argue that our choices and actions are pre-ordained (i.e. we are like pre-programmed robots) and that we cannot, therefore, be held responsible for them. Only if our actions are freely chosen can we be held morally responsible for them.

A moral situation is one in which the individual can choose a particular course of action. A non-moral situation is one in which the individual has no choice or has their choice dictated to them (i.e. the course of action is determined in both cases):

"I am not to blame if I cannot draw a round square."	*"I am not to blame if I am forced to commit a crime at gunpoint."*
no choice	choice dictated

Responding to the Free Will Problem

Biblical and rabbinic literature don't systematically analyse philosophical issues, including the concept of free will. The Bible is clear that God has a role in determining human affairs, and equally clear that, in most cases, human beings can choose between right and wrong. This contradiction does not seem to bother the biblical writer(s), and thus the Bible provides no clear solution to the free will problem. Some rabbinic sources indicate an awareness that divine providence and human choice might be contradictory, but no systematic solutions are articulated.

Solving the free will problem –e specially the problem of divine foreknowledge – was a major aspect of medieval Jewish philosophy, which offered an array of possible theories about what God knows and doesn't know. For example, Gersonides suggested that God knows the choices from which we will choose but doesn't know the specific choice we will make.

Gersonides' position – seemingly radical because of the limitations it puts on God's capabilities–pales in comparison to the unique position of the Hasidic leader known as the Izbicer Rebbe. He claimed that there is no philosophical problem related to Free will, because humans don't have free will. While humans have control over their thoughts and intentions, God is the active cause of every human action. This sort of determinism is often referred to as "soft determinism." "Hard determinism" refers to the idea that even thoughts, intentions, and feelings are predetermined.

Modern Jewish thinkers also address the problem of free will, though more often than not, instead of solving the problem of *how* it can exist, they discuss when and where it does exist.

In many ways, free will in the modern period is an even more significant philosophical issue, as contemporary life emphasizes personal autonomy in a way that traditional societies didn't.

Summary: Free Will

- Free will is the ability to make moral decisions, choosing between right and wrong.
- According to the Genesis account, humans were gifted free will by God.
- Humans are the only creatures that have been gifted free will.
- Humans are the pinnacle of creation because no other creature possesses free will.
- We have a yetzer tov (moral conscience) which guides our Free will.
- If we misuse free will, this can lead to suffering as a result of sin.
- The Genesis account also teaches us that the consequence of misusing free will; when Adam and Eve chose to disobey God He punished them by inflicting suffering.

4 SIN

Judaism teaches that human beings are not born sinful. There is no belief that humanity carries the sin of our ancestors or share in some kind of collective wrongdoing. For something to be a 'sin' it must be an intentional act that is understood as wrong and a result of free will.

The Hebrew word for sin is *chet* which literally means something that 'goes astray' or off the path. It's important to remember that whilst it is easy to walk off a path, it's equally possible to get back on it – and Judaism has a clear process to return. This process is called *Teshuvah* or 'return'.

The Torah has numerous examples of characters who are flawed and have made mistakes. But these show that we can still be good people, even if we sometimes act in ways that conflict with goodness. Our characters are shaped by how we respond to our failures rather than the failures themselves.

Sin is literally understood as an act of wrong doing, so anything that goes against God's commandments - the 613 mitzvot – would be seen as a sin. It is believed that are two kinds of sin: those against God and those against people – which some people subdivide to include sins against the self.

An example of a sin against God would be blaspheming i.e., speaking about God in a disrespectful way, or breaking Shabbat i.e., failing to observe the Sabbath. An example of sin against people would be stealing, or even *lashon harah* – gossiping and lying.

Sin against others is considered to be more serious than sins against God; as God is almighty He is not damaged by sin, whereas humans are clearly hurt by sin. Therefore, whilst Judaism teaches that sin against God can be forgiven through prayer it is not as simple to gain forgiveness for hurting others.

Summary: Sin

- There are 3 types of sin, sin against yourself (failing to get help for addiction), sin against others (gossip/lashon harah) and sin against God (blasphemy).
- Sin against others is the worst because God cannot be damaged by sin.
- It is doing something that goes against the 613 mitzvot (the Torah i.e. law).
- Humans are given free will by God, they can control whether they sin and choose between right and wrong.
- For something to be a sin it has to be done of free will and they have to understand it is a sin.
- Sin is going astray and it is called *chet* in Hebrew.
- It is possible to return to the law after sinning, through the process of teshuvah – which involves prayer and giving to charity.
- Forgiveness for sin is possible if one makes up for what they have done i.e. restoration.

Rosh Hashanah

Rosh Hashanah is the Jewish New Year celebration which commemorates the creation of the world. However, the Talmud (book of Jewish law) calls Rosh Hashanah the 'Day of Judgment' since, on this day, God balances a person's good deeds against their bad deeds from the last year, and decides what their fate will be for the coming year. The Talmud says that God writes down these actions, so it is customary to greet others at this time with the words, 'May you be inscribed in the Book of Life for a good year.'

Rosh Hashanah is a day of accountability, so Jews spend a lot of time reflecting on the year gone by and thinking what they can do better in the future. A lot of time is spent in the synagogue as there are special services that emphasis God's kingship.

In the synagogue the *shofar*, a ram's horn, is blown 100 times. There are three different types of trumpet blast which are to encourage people to wake up to the consequences of their sin, and to remind them to repent and be sorry for their sins.

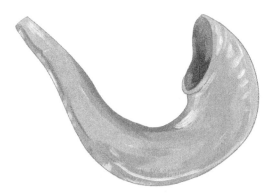

As well as a service in the synagogue, families carry out traditions at home beginning with a special meal. The **kiddush** is recited before traditional foods sweetened with honey, apples and carrots are served, symbolising sweetness, blessings, abundance, and the hope for a sweet year ahead. The first night's meal begins with apple dipped in honey. **Challah**, the bread usually eaten on the Sabbath (not braided as at regular meals but instead baked in a circle - a wish that the coming year will roll around smoothly without unhappiness or sorrow) is also dipped in honey before eating.

After the meal, Jews visit a body of water or pond, containing live fish, to symbolically "**cast away**" their sins into the river. This is called the *tashlikh* ceremony. The fish's dependence on water symbolises the Jews dependence on God.

This leads into ten days of repentance, or 'ten days of returning', until Yom Kippur – at which point the Book of Life will be slammed shut. So during this time, everyone must try to make amends for what they have done wrong and say sorry to those they have hurt.

According to Jewish tradition, only sins against God can be atoned for through confession, regret and promising not to repeat the action. Sins against other people can be atoned for only once the wrong has been made right — restitution has been paid for a financial crime, for example, and forgiveness received from the victim.

Yom Kippur

Yom Kippur ends the days of repentance, and God decision regard the year ahead for each person has been sealed in the Book of Life. Jews turn from asking each other for forgiveness to asking God for forgiveness for promises broken to Him.

Yom Kippur begins at sunset, but before it starts, a meal must be eaten. Candles are lit and a 25-hour fast begins. There is an evening service at the synagogue, Men put on prayer shawls and the cantor begins the *'Kol Nidre'*. This prayer asks God for forgiveness for vows they have failed to keep in the past year; it is repeated 3 times, each time in a louder voice. The Kol Nidre emphasises the importance in keeping vows, as violating an oath is one of the worst sins.

The following the day, everyone goes to the synagogue however, there is no blowing of the **Shofar** and there are series of prohibitions:

1. Eating and drinking
2. Anointing with perfumes or lotions
3. Marital relations
4. Washing
5. Wearing leather shoes

It is believed that to fast on Yom Kippur is to emulate the angels in heaven, who do not eat, drink, or wash.

One of the most important part of the Yom Kippur service is the *'Vidui'* or confession. The confessions serve to help reflect on one's misdeeds and to confess them verbally is part of the formal repentance in asking God's forgiveness. But this is not about individual guilt, the confessions are said in the plural – 'We are guilty' – reflecting that Judaism is a religion of community.

As Yom Kippur ends, at the last hour a service called *'Ne'ila'* offers a final opportunity for repentance. It is the only service of the year during which the doors to the Ark (where the Torah scrolls are stored) remain open from the beginning to end of the service, signifying that the gates of Heaven are open at this time. The service closes with the verse, said 7 times, "The Lord is our God." The Shofar is sounded once and the congregation proclaims - "Next year in Jerusalem."

5 THE EXODUS

The Exodus

Exodus comes from a Greek word meaning "exit" or "departure." The Exodus happened around either 1240 or 1440 BC. Tradition holds that Moses wrote the book of Exodus.

The book of Exodus records the history of Israel's enslavement to Pharaoh and their freedom through a deliverer that God raised up. This deliverer was named Moses, and Moses was given the task of leading his people out of Egypt to the promised land, the land of Canaan. This event was called the Exodus.

Exodus reveals the God who saves his people. From Exodus we come to understand that God is actively involved in history. He hears prayer. He answers. He saves, but God does things in his own way, in his own time, and for his own glory. Exodus teaches us what we should expect from God. Exodus gives us reason to trust God in difficult times. Exodus shows how God is at work to save the world from sin, death, and the devil.

The Story of Exodus

The story begins with Israel as an oppressed people in Egypt. Israel was a foreign people who came to Egypt during a great famine. The pharaoh welcomed them. Years went by. A new pharaoh ascended to the throne, and this pharaoh was unaware of the history of all Joseph did to help Egypt. The pharaoh grew worried by the size of Israel's population, so he decided to do two things. The first was to force the Israelites into slave labour. The second was to mandate the killing of all newborn male children. It was into this situation that Moses was born.

In an attempt to spare Moses, his mother placed him in a basket and sent him down the Nile River. Farther down the river, Pharaoh's daughter was bathing and accidentally discovered the baby Moses. She recognized the child as belonging to one of the Israelites, but she had compassion on the boy and adopted him.

After many years and a new pharaoh, God met Moses in a burning bush. There God called him to be his prophet and lead his people to the land of Canaan, but there was a problem. The new pharaoh still held God's people in slavery. When Moses approached

Pharaoh about freeing the Israelites, Pharaoh refused to let them go. Thus, God intervened by sending a series of plagues:

1. **The Plague of Blood:** God turned the water of the River Nile into blood so that the fish died and the water stank. All the water in Egypt was turned into blood.

2. **The Plague of Frogs:** Egypt was overrun with frogs - there were frogs in the beds, frogs in the ovens, and frogs jumping on the people.

3. **The Plague of Lice:** Dust was turned into lice which crawled on people and animals. (The Bible calls this The Plague of Gnats, but in Judaism the accepted translation of the Hebrew word *Kinim* is lice).

4. **The Plague of Flies:** Swarms of flies arrived in Egypt and poured into Pharaoh's palace, the houses of his officials, and all over the land. (The Hebrew word here is *orov* meaning mixture and in Jewish tradition this refers to a mixture of wild animals.)

5. **The Plague on Livestock:** All animals belonging to the Egyptians died - horses, donkeys, camels, cattle, sheep and goats.

6. **The Plague of Boils:** Festering boils broke out on the Egyptian people and their livestock.

7. **The Plague of Hail:** The worst hailstorm ever to hit Egypt struck, beating down crops growing in the fields and even killing people and animals caught in it.

8. **The Plague of Locusts:** A swarm of locusts settled in Egypt and devoured anything left growing after the hail.

9. **The Plague of Darkness:** Egypt became totally dark for three days.

10. **The plague on the firstborn:** The death of every Egyptian firstborn.

To avoid the final plague, each Hebrew household was told to take an unblemished, male lamb, look after it, and slaughter it at twilight four days later. Blood from the lamb was to be brushed on the door frames. This would tell the avenging angel that it was an Israelite home and to 'pass over'. Then the families were to roast the lamb and eat it with bitter herbs and unleavened bread. Every bit of the lamb had to be eaten and any remaining bones burned.

At midnight every Egyptian firstborn - from the firstborn of Pharaoh to the firstborn of the prisoner in his cell - and even of the livestock - was struck down by the angel. The Egyptians were terrified and demanded Pharaoh banish the Israelites there and then. Finally, the Pharoah admitted defeat and let Moses and his people go.

As Moses and the Israelites began to leave, Pharaoh, still unwilling to admit defeat, changed his mind. He and the Egyptian army pursued the Israelites up to the Red Sea. Moses and the people had come to what looked like a dead end, but God was with them. Through a great miracle, God spread the waters of the Red Sea so that Israel could walk across on dry land. When the Egyptians tried to walk across the parted sea, God released the waves, drowning the Egyptian army.

The Israelites leave Egypt and make their way to Mount Sinai, where God gives His laws to Moses. During this 'wandering' time, God provides the Hebrews with sustenance in the form of 'manna'. At Mount Sinai, God makes a covenant with the nation of Israel and the generations to come: because He rescued them from Egypt, Israel is to observe His rules. God speaks the Ten Commandments directly to the whole nation of Israel, and He relays specific ordinances to Moses on the mountain.

Summary: The Exodus

- Gods speaks to Moses through burning bush – asking him to deliver the Hebrews from slavery
- Moses visits Pharaoh, requesting he release the Jews from slavery but he says no
- Moses warns Pharaoh before the 10 plagues are sent by God.
- Hebrews mark their door posts with lambs' blood to make angel of death pass over.
- Pharaoh allows the Hebrews to leave, Moses leads them to the Red Sea but Pharoah changes his mind, he sends soldiers to bring the Hebrews back.
- Moses parts the Red Sea, allowing the Hebrews to escape and crushes the Pharaoh's soldiers in the water.
- God provided 'manna' (food) during the wandering time
- Moses leads Hebrews to Mount Sinai, there he received the commandments and the Mosaic covenant was made.

Pesach

The festival of Pesach has been celebrated to remember the Exodus. Although this event took place more than 4,000 years ago, for Jews it remains the most important example of God's power. The festival of Pesach is a reliving of the events of the Exodus story.

The Seder meal

Although there are services in the synagogue, the most important part of the festival takes place in the home with the **Seder** meal. Seder literally translates as 'order' and the during the meal, the story of Exodus is told from a book called the **Haggadah**. The Haggadah is a 14 step story of the Jewish experience both of slavery and redemption, but it also contains songs, blessings, psalms and questions.

The meal starts with the blessing of red wine or red grape juice. Four glasses of wine/grape juice are drunk to remind Jews of God's four promises (covenant) to Moses. The Seder plate has seven items all of which have a symbolic meaning. They remind the Jews of part of the Exodus:

- **Matzah bread**. Three loaves of Matzah, or unleavened bread. This helps the Jews feel solidarity with their ancestors, who were slaves.
- **Salt water**. Some of the Seder food is dipped into salt water. Salt water calls to mind the tears of the slaves, and also the water of the Red Sea which once crossed meant the Jews were really free.
- **Charoset**. This is a mixture of almonds, apples mixed with cinnamon and wine. This represents the mud that the Jews had to make into bricks when they were slaves.
- **Bitter herbs**. These represent the bitterness of the slavery, but the green reminds them that after the tears of slavery came the freedom of the escape.
- **Karpas**. Karpas are green leafy vegetables. It serves as a symbol of the wonderful bounty of vegetables and fruits in the springtime harvest. It also represents the period of Jewish flourishing before the period of Egyptian slavery began.

You can see that many of the items on the Seder plate are reminders of both slavery and freedom, the Seder meal is about the passage from slavery to freedom. The next two items are not connected with slavery in Egypt and recall practices which have long since ceased. Jews have not performed animal sacrifices since the temple was destroyed.

- **A roasted shank bone** to represent the lamb which was slaughtered in the temple until it was destroyed in 70 CE.
- **A roasted egg** which recalls the sacrifice in the temple for the Passover.

Children are central to Passover proceedings and symbolise the continuity of the Jewish people. Customs are designed to hold their attention. There's the hunt for the *afikomen*, where a piece of matzoh is hidden which children have to find and hold 'ransom' until a reward is given. There are also four questions that the youngest child must ask, these are designed to be Socratic – helping children to develop their understanding.

A fifth cup of wine is poured and stands undrunk on the table. This is for the prophet *Elijah* as it is hoped that he will return and announce the return of Messiah at Pesach. The door will be left slightly ajar for the same reason.

Understanding the relevance of the Exodus today

There is almost no historical evidence that the Exodus ever happened. For example, there is no mention of it in Egyptian sources. What is interesting is that Passover is not meant to confirm that this event really took place. For Jews, the Seder is rather an opportunity to relive a story: a chance to feel what it means to be oppressed and to feel what it means to be oppressed and to be free from oppression, and to do that with family and friends from within the Jewish community.

Exodus is a book about freedom from slavery. Whilst, it may be a story set in the past, slavery still exists today in many forms. Some slavery is imposed from the outside, such as human trafficking or even systemic racism. Whereas other slavery is within us, such as addiction to money or the pursuit of notoriety. Exodus answers both. Exodus gives words of hope to people suffering from injustice and to those suffering from their own demons. The experience of slavery that breaks and crushes slaves does not destroy free people. It evokes feelings of repulsion and determination to help others escape that state.

It is a living story, shared with every Jewish person around the world, and with all those from previous generations who have participated in the same process. During the ritual, all Jewish people become one with their ancestors. Telling the story and discussing it in the present are what makes the Seder important: it is accessible to everyone no matter what their status.

The laws handed to the Jewish people on Mount Sinai also transformed their system. Instead of God being responsible for the administration of justice, clear laws were given to protect the weak and poor: honest weights and measures, interest-free loans to the poor, leaving part of the crops in the field for the stranger, the orphan, and the widow, treating the alien stranger as a native citizen — these are all applications of the Exodus principle to living in this world.

Summary: How the Exodus is observed

- Pesach means the 'feast of Unleavened Bread.'
- It commemorates the Exodus and God leading his people out of Egypt.
- Begins on 15 Nisan (March/April)
- The festival allows them to keep the story alive and remember that God sent Moses to rescue them from slavery.
- God helped Jews in the past and this gives assurance he will help in the future.
- It is a time to teach children about the Covenant and to thank God for looking after them.
- At the end of the Seder meal the family propose a toast - "Next year in Jerusalem" – this symbolises hope that the Jewish nation will be united and have their homeland.

Preparation
- House is thoroughly cleaned and all leaven removed.
- Children and father hunt for crumbs and then burn them.
- Orthodox also use different dishes and utensils for the duration.

Celebrations

- Ceremonial meal called Seder is held on the first night.
  - Symbolic items of food and drink are placed on the table
    - Matzah
    - Shank bone
    - Roasted egg etc.
  - A special cup is placed on the table for Elijah who is expected to herald the coming of the Messiah.
  - Kiddush prayer said by father. Youngest child asks questions. Story retold.
  - Father reads from Haggadah while foods are eaten in set way.
  - Hymns and prayers are sung remind people of the first Exodus.
- Orthodox Jews repeat this on the second night as well.
- People will invite others to join them for the Seder meal as Moses had told people to invite their neighbour to eat the lamb.

6 COVENANT

The Covenant

The word covenant is best seen as a way of understanding God's relationship with humanity. It can be understood as **an agreement between two parties**. Both parties to the agreement have to fulfil obligations or duties if the covenant is to be considered binding.

A covenant is **a commitment** of love and creates a relationship that is fundamentally different from that of a contract. Covenants in Judaism can only be established and sealed by an oath. The oath is so important in a covenant that the word oath is sometimes used as a synonym for covenant. The covenant with God is described as an 'everlasting covenant' (***brit olam***). This describes the view that **God will never break his covenant agreement with the Jewish people**, even if, from time to time, they fail to fulfil their covenant obligations and break His laws.

Jews are sometimes referred to as the '**Chosen People**'. This description has caused some problems because it gives the impression that Jews are in some way superior as a nation, and has led to many acts of anti-Semitism. Being chosen does not mean that Jews think they are better than other people; it means God has places an obligation on them - **chosen for responsibility, and not for superiority.**

God made covenants with His people throughout the Jewish scriptures:

Adam

In the Garden of Eden, God promised to provide what humans needed whilst Adam was to tend the garden and refrain from eating from the tree of the knowledge of good and evil. As long as he obeyed these terms he would live, otherwise he would die.

Noah

The 'Noahchide Covenant' was established after the flood when God promised to never again destroy human beings. God set out seven rules that all people were to keep. These laws are the prohibition of idolatry, murder, theft, sexual immorality, blasphemy, eating flesh of an animal whilst it is still alive and the requirement of maintaining courts to provide legal recourse (an action that can be taken by an individual or a corporation to attempt to remedy a legal difficulty).

Abraham

Jewish tradition believes that Abraham, who became the first Jew, was born in the city of Ur in Mesopotamia in approximately 1800 BCE. His father was a man who made his living by selling idols, but from his early childhood, Abraham became convinced of the presence in the world of a higher power. He came to believe that the universe was the creative work of a single divine Creator. He began to spread this belief to other people and in doing so became the first believer in the idea of monotheism (belief in one God).

The Torah in Genesis 12 describes how God spoke to Abraham and commanded him to abandon his old life in Mesopotamia and to travel to the land of Canaan – later to be known as **Israel**. There, God promised Abraham that he would be the founder of a great nation – giving him as many descendants as 'stars in the sky.' God would bless him and would protect him from any harmful nations.

As a sign of this 'Abrahamic covenant', all males were to be circumcised – a practice still continued today through the *brit Milah* ceremony.

Abraham was subjected to ten tests of faith to convince God that he was worthy to accept the covenant. Obeying the command to leave home was the first of these tests. The last was the test of sacrificing his son, Isaac.

The Torah records how, at the age of 75, Abraham, together with his wife Sarah, his nephew Lot and all his household, left his birthplace in Mesopotamia to travel to Canaan, which God had promised Abraham's descendants.

Moses

The Mosaic Covenant was made with Moses at Mount Sinai. God reaffirmed that He would be faithful to the Jewish people and would protect them. He gave Moses the Ten Commandments which the people were to keep as their side of the covenant.

1. I am the Lord your God
2. You shall have no other gods before Me
3. You shall not take the name of the Lord your God in vain
4. Observe the Sabbath day to keep it holy
5. Honour you father and mother
6. You shall not murder
7. You shall not commit adultery
8. You shall not steal
9. You shall not bear false witness against your neighbour
10. You shall not covet your neighbour's wife

The first four commandments refer to the relationship between a person and God. This is how people should worship and respect God, remembering what He has done for them.

The other six commandments are to do with the relationship between people. They show how God expects a community of His people to behave. If their relationship with God is right, their relationship with each other should be right too. The last commandment shows how God looks at the heart and sees a person's motives.

Summary: Covenant

- A covenant is a solemn agreement to engage in or refrain from a specified action. In the context of Judaism it is an agreement between God and human beings.

Abrahamic
God side
- Give Abraham descendants who would become a great nation.
- Give them their own land.
- Protect and look after his people.

Abraham side
- Abraham and his descendants and to worship God and only God.
- Move to land of Canaan.
- All males had to be circumcised as a sign of the covenant.

Mosaic
God side
- The Jews would be a free nation.
- Delivered from slavery and led to the Promised Land.
- They would be the chosen people forever.

Moses side
- Worship only God.
- Follow his commands in return for His help and love.

Brit Milah

The birth of a baby in Judaism is celebrated as life is a gift from God. Girls have a naming ceremony in the synagogue, but for boys it is different. God told Abraham that all males should be circumcised as a sign of the covenant He made with him, that that practice is still observed today.

Brit Milah (pr. *breet meelah*) is the term given to male circumcision – the removal of the baby boy's foreskin when he is eight days old. Judaism does not permit female circumcision – which is more accurately known as female genital mutilation.

Circumcision is practised by many peoples in the world but it is only for the Jewish people that it is a sign of their acceptance of their relationship with God. As described in Genesis 17: 9–14, where it originated from the time of Abraham, circumcision is an external symbol of the covenant. Brit Milah should take place, in accordance with Leviticus 12: 3 on the eighth day after birth, even if this falls on Shabbat or Yom Kippur. The only factor that allows the postponement of the circumcision is the baby's health.

As previously mentioned, being Jewish is a matter of birth except in the case of a convert, so circumcision does not turn a baby into a Jew. According to **halachah** an uncircumcised Jew is still a Jew if he has a Jewish mother.

A circumcision is an occasion for celebration for the family and the community. Today the preferred place for this to take place is at home. The ceremony is performed by a **mohel**, a person who is medically qualified to do it, on the eighth day after birth. Appropriate short prayers and blessings are recited. It is a great honour to be asked to hold the baby during the ceremony, or to be the one who hands the baby to the mohel, this person is called the **sandek**. Whilst it is preferable to have a **minyan** (a group of 10 men) for this event, it is not a requirement. The ceremony ends with the **kiddush** over a glass of wine.

Some circumcisions occur in hospital where the ceremony is curtailed, but the essential blessings can still be recited.

Circumcision has become a controversial issue worldwide with claims that it causes unnecessary pain and is an infringement of the child's rights. However, while the health benefits are very evenly balanced it is important to remember that it is not being done for health reasons but as an act of faith indicating a belief in God and in the covenant between God and Abraham. It is carried out even by the non-observant. It is a religious right upheld by human-rights legislation. Those who perform the circumcision are highly skilled after long training and there is a minimum of upset to the infant.

Summary: One way the Covenant is observed

Brit Milah

- 8 days after he is born, a boy has the foreskin of his penis removed.
- Sandek holds baby.
- A moshel, a trained circumciser, is employed to carry out the operation.
- After a prayer of intent, the foreskin is removed with a quick stroke of the knife.
- The father of the child says a prayer of blessing to God.
- The child is then given a name.
- A blessing is said over a glass of wine, some of which is dropped onto the baby's lips.
- The father drinks some of the wine and the rest is sent to the mother, who is in another room, to drink. Reform Jews may not separate the woman.

Shabbat

God rested from His work on the seventh day of creation. This is **Shabbat,** the day of rest, which is described in **Genesis 2: 1–3.** By resting on Shabbat and observing the laws relating to Shabbat, Jews proclaim their belief that God created the world, and that after completing His work, He stopped. When Jews observe Shabbat, they are in a sense imitating God as they too stop their work for one day. They are also keeping God's fourth commandment, *'Remember the Sabbath day to keep it holy'* **(Exodus 20: 8–11)**, which links with the creation narrative.

Not only does Shabbat appear in the Ten Commandments, but it is also repeated more often in the Torah than any other commandment.

According to the Book of Genesis, first there was darkness, and then came light. And each day is announced with the phrase 'And the evening and the morning were the third day', and so on. Thus, Jews take the viewpoint that the night time *precedes* the daytime. Shabbat thus **begins at sunset on Friday and end at sunset on Saturday**. This means that preparations for Shabbat are done beforehand, as no work e.g. cooking or shopping, may be done on Shabbat itself. There are 39 forbidden types of work on Shabbat which are defined in the Jewish text called the **Mishnah.** These are called the 39 forbidden **melachot** which were jobs that were necessary for building the portable Temple or **Tabernacle** that the Israelites built in the desert after they had come out of Egypt. Melachot include baking, lighting a fire, sewing and writing. They are not single tasks but are broad categories. For example sewing involves joining two materials permanently together by means of a third substance. Therefore it also includes stapling bits of paper together. Similarly writing would include word processing on the computer.

There are also tasks that reflect the nature of the modern world that are forbidden on Shabbat. These include driving on Shabbat, using the telephone, watching television, playing on the computer, taking photographs, switching on electricity. Orthodox and Reform Jews have different traditions in observing Shabbat e.g. Reform Jews consider it acceptable to drive to synagogue while observant Orthodox Jews meticulously keep all the melachot. Irrespective of the various traditions of Judaism, all Jews try to make the atmosphere in their homes on Shabbat special and different from the rest of the week, and tend to make it a time for relaxing and spending time with the family.

Preparation for Shabbat involves observant Jews in preparing all the Shabbat food beforehand. Food is kept hot by being placed on a metal sheet over the hot stove. The house is cleaned to welcome Shabbat and time switches are set to accommodate the turning off and on of lights. Adults and children get dressed in their best clothes and the Shabbat table is carefully made, with a special and different tablecloth, on which the best cutlery and crockery are placed.

Just before sunset the mother or woman of the house lights two (white) Shabbat candles. As she does so, she beckons with her arms to welcome Shabbat into her home, and covers her eyes to recite a blessing[2]. Observant Jews will go to the synagogue for the special evening service. As people leave the synagogue, they greet each other with 'Good Shabbos' or 'Shabbat Shalom' which literally means 'have a peaceful Shabbat'.

At home, the father blesses the children and recites **Kiddush,** a blessing over wine. After everyone has washed their hands, the father or man of the house recites the blessing for bread over the **challot.**

The two challot represent the manna, the miracle food which the Israelites ate during their journey through the desert (Exodus 16: 14– 18). The manna appeared outside the doors of their tents on every day except Shabbat. To accommodate this, God gave them a double portion on Friday. This is represented by the double loaves at the Shabbat meal. The challot are usually plaited or braided loaves. The singular of challot is challah (pronounced *chala,* sounding *'ch'* as in *'loch'),* which is a sweet, golden type of bread.

After the blessing, the bread is cut and passed round for each person to take. The meal then begins. The meal is different from any other meal of the week in that grandparents, other relatives or friends may be invited as guests, and it is a relaxed, unhurried meal. Guests who wish to fully observe the laws of Shabbat and who do not live close by, will be invited to stay overnight until the end of Shabbat. Jewish families look forward to this weekly opportunity just to be together and enjoy each other's company.

Shabbat morning is the time for synagogue as the Shabbat morning service, called **shacharit,** is held. This is an altogether longer service than the weekday services, since in addition to the longer-than-usual weekday shacharit there is an additional service known as **mussaf.** A part of the Torah, called a **sidra,** is read from the **Sefer Torah** each Shabbat so that the entire scroll is completed during the course of the year. After the service a communal **kiddush** is held in the hall attached to the synagogue for all the congregants.

When it is dark enough for three stars to be seen in the sky on Saturday night, Shabbat is over. Shabbat ends with the **Havdalah** ceremony in which four blessings are recited. The first blessing is over a cup of wine; the second is done over fragrant spices which are kept in a special decorated holder. Spices commonly used are cloves and cinnamon. The spices are smelled to refresh the soul with the departure of the Shabbat spirit. The third blessing is recited over the light of the plaited candle. This candle has several wicks and their kindling shows that fire can now be made. This marks the distinction between Shabbat and weekdays.

The final blessing is the Havdalah blessing itself. Havdalah means 'separation' and this is the blessing over the separation of the holy day from the work day. After this blessing, the wine is drunk and a few drops of wine are used to extinguish the flame from the candle.

7 JUDGEMENT

"Judaism is a religion of hope, and its great rituals of repentance and atonement are part of that hope. We are not condemned to live endlessly with the mistakes and errors of our past."
- Rabbi Jonathan Sacks (1948-2020)

The Torah tends to describe immediate reward and punishment, rather than future judgement after death. For example, in the book of Genesis, Lot's wife was immediately turned into a pillar of salt for looking back at the city of Sodom. Additionally, there are some places in the Torah that imply death is the end of everything. When Adam is being punished by God for committing the first sin he is told: *the sweat of your face you shall eat bread until you return to the ground, for out of it you were taken; you are dust, and to dust you will return.'* This leads some Jews to believe there is no life after death that judgement occurs in this life – God judges people each year on Rosh Hashanah and seals His judgement in the book of life on Yom Kippur.

However, in later Scripture another idea emerges: in the book of Ecclesiastes it states '... *the dust returns to the earth as it was, and the breath returns to God who gave it.'* It is teachings like this that led to the development of ideas about a final judgment after death.

Some Jews believe that they will be judged as soon as they die. They believe that God judges the persons soul and decides its eternal destiny in the afterlife. Others believe that the Day of Judgement, or Yawm ad-Din, will occur after the coming of the Messiah and that he and God will judge each soul. On this day, some Jews believe that the dead will be resurrected so that they can be judged, whilst others believe only the good will be resurrected.

There are also different ideas about what punishment or reward might mean. Many think that the righteous will be rewarded with a place in paradise – **Gan Eden** – which is a place of sunshine where people of all nations will sit and eat together when the Messianic Age comes. Others believe that Gan Eden is not a physical place, but the righteous will experience nearness to God.

For the wicked it is possible that souls could be sent to Sheol or Gehinnom. Sheol is a place of waiting where souls are cleansed and purified whereas Gehinnom is a place to be punished and a place of torment. Some believe that the souls of those who have committed serious acts of evil - for example, people who have committed murder - will never move on from this place of torment as they cannot be changed for the better. Whereas others believe that there is no physical place of torment, but that the wicked will simply have their souls destroyed entirely.

The impact of belief in judgement

It's important to note that for those who believe in a final judgement after death, it's still the actions in this life that will affect it. Therefore, Jewish people would still seek to follow the 613 mitzvot and maintain a relationship with God - awareness of an eternal reward is a powerful motivator to follow the rules. The Talmud likens this life to the eve before Sabbath, and the afterlife to the Sabbath; suggesting that whilst the afterlife is important, it is still necessary to prepare for it.

However, as the Torah does not explicitly refer to the afterlife many Jews prefer to focus on how they live in this world. The 613 mitzvot – or commandments - are about faithfulness to God in the here and now, how we treat others, and maintain justice. They are not about the afterlife.

Summary: Judgement

- There is no one understanding about judgment in Judaism.
- Some people believe that God judges each soul, and decides its eternal destiny when people die.
- Some believe that people are divided into three groups: the righteous, the wicked, and those in between.
- Jews have different ideas about what punishment or reward might mean, e.g. Gan Eden is a paradise after death, and some believe in a place of punishment called Gehinnom.
- Others say there is no literal paradise or hell, instead the righteous experience nearness to God, or shame depending on how well they have observed the 613 commandments.
- For some Judgment is associated with the resurrection of the dead, the Messianic age and the end of the world.
- Some believe God judges people every year at Rosh Hashanah, and seals His judgements in the Book of Life at Yom Kippur.
- The Torah tends to describe immediate reward and punishment, rather than future judgement.

8 MESSIAH

Messiah means 'anointed one', as were the kings and high priests of ancient Israel. To be anointed by God meant to be given special powers to carry out specific tasks in Israel's history:

- The High Priest was anointed so that he could carry out his scared duties. One of these duties was to offer sacrifices to God on behalf of the people. The book of Leviticus in the Torah sets out in great detail how, why and when sacrifices were to be offered.
- Kings were also described as being God's anointed. As the book of Samuel describes: Then Samuel took a flask of oil and poured it on his head and kissed him and said, *"Has not the LORD anointed you to be prince over his people Israel? And you shall reign over the people of the LORD and you will save them from the hand of their surrounding enemies. And this shall be the sign to you that the LORD has anointed you to be prince over his heritage."*

Jewish people do not believe that the Messiah has yet come, if only because the world is so obviously not at peace and so many of our problems remain unsolved. But the idea remains a hope and an expectation, one which has often been disappointed over the last two thousand years but to which all Jews continue to look forward. The Messianic idea does not originate in the Torah but it gradually develops throughout the time of the prophets:

Malachi

"'See, I will send my messenger, who will prepare the way before me. Then suddenly the Lord you are seeking will come to his temple; the messenger of the covenant, whom you desire, will come,' says the LORD Almighty."

Micah

"But you, O Bethlehem Ephrathah, who are too little to be among the clans of Judah, from you shall come forth for me one who is to be ruler in Israel, whose coming forth is from of old, from ancient days."

Isaiah

"For unto us a Child is born, Unto us a Son is given; And the government will be upon His shoulder. And His name will be called Wonderful, Counselor, Mighty God, Everlasting Father, Prince of Peace. Of the increase of His government and peace There will be no end, Upon the throne of David and over His kingdom, To order it and establish it with judgment and justice From that time forward, even forever. The zeal of the LORD of hosts will perform this."

Orthodox teaching about the Messiah

Orthodox Judaism teaches that at some time in the future, a Messiah, a descendant of King David, will come but he will create a state even greater than David's golden age. When that time comes, peace will reign on earth and, as described particularly in Isaiah:

'the wolf also shall dwell with the lamb, and the leopard shall lie down with the kid; and the calf and the young lion and the fatling together; and a little child shall lead them ... They shall not hurt or destroy in all my holy mountain; for the earth shall be full of the knowledge of the Lord, as the waters cover the sea' (Isaiah 9: 6–7).

The Messiah would be a man who, at the end of days, would lead the Jewish people back to the land of Israel. He will deliver the Jewish people from their enemies, restoring the homeland and the Temple in Jerusalem.

There have been many people who have claimed to be the Messiah during the last two thousand years, but all were eventually found to be false. One of the most famous was Shabbatai Zevi in 1666 who had a great following throughout the Middle East and even as far west as England. There were even bets being made on the London Stock Exchange on the likelihood of him being the real thing. However, he was arrested by the Turkish authorities and offered the choice of converting to Islam or immediate execution. He chose conversion. The disappointment among the masses of Jewish people who had fervently believed in him was enormous. It had a devastating effect upon their morale and many gave up their Judaism.

There have been many other false messiahs who managed to attract followers only to be disappointed by events. This always produced local political unrest and the governments of the countries in which these false messiahs operated were anxious to put down the movements from Roman times right up to the eighteenth century.

It is for these reasons that the **Talmud** warns us not to try to guess or attempt to calculate when the Messiah will come because such hopes just lead to disappointment and disillusion of which there have been many examples over the last two thousand years.

Orthodox Jews believe that the Messiah will only arrive when Israel repents and when everyone keeps the Sabbath perfectly. Only then will the world be back to what it is meant to be. Hasidic Jews believe that there is one person born in each generation who could potentially be the Messiah. Whereas other Jews say that it is impossible to tell when the Messiah will come, and that everyone must make up their own minds.

Reform teaching about the Messiah

Many **Reform Jews** do not believe that the Messiah is a single person. Rather they believe that the 'Messianic Age' refers to a time of world peace. Instead of placing the responsibility for this on an individual, they believe that everyone must work together to bring peace. They believe that the 'rebuilding of the Temple' is a metaphor for the Messianic Age where there is peace all people know God and follow his commandments. As a result, Reform Jews pray for redemption rather than for a 'redeemer'.

Summary: Messiah

Orthodox
- An actual person will be the Messiah.
- He will not be God, but a special human being.
- He will deliver the Jews from their enemies and restore the homeland.
- He will be a descendant of King David and would create a state greater than David's golden age.
- He will set up a perfect kingdom of peace on Earth in the future.
- He will restore the Temple in Jerusalem and their obedience to The Torah.
- They state that this concept has always been part of Judaism and see Torah references to 'the End of Days' as directly referring to Messianic Age. They say that the concept itself was probably too abstract to be understood by ordinary people of the time and that's why it is not specifically mentioned in the Torah.
- Some read message as literal – that the laws of nature will change and beasts will no longer seek prey and lambs and wolves would lie down together.
- Other's see this as an allegory for a time of peace and prosperity.
- Hasidic Jews believe that he will perform miracles and demonstrate supernatural power.

Reform
- Reform Jews do not think of him as a real person.
- There will be a particular time or age in the future.
- All people will live on Earth in harmony.
- All people together bring it – paradise on earth
- Jews and Gentiles (non-Jews) will share peace, justice and kindness.
- Some believe the Messianic Kingdom has already been established in The State of Israel in 1948.

9 OLAM HA BA

Olam Ha Ba means the 'World to Come' which is in contrast with Olam Ha zeh which is this world. It is sometimes seen as the end of this world, however there is no clear agreement about this in Judaism which leaves room for personal opinion. Some see it as a physical existence after death, some see it as a spiritual state, and others associate it with the future Messianic Age.

Why is there a difference?

There is little teaching about life after death in Jewish holy books, and beliefs have developed over the centuries and in different places. This had led to differences between Jews in their idea about life after death or the end times. This lack of dogma is one of the reasons that many Jews believe that they should focus on their life and actions now and not spend time focusing on something that may or may not happen.

Reminder

Tenakh – Jewish Holy Book

Torah – the first five books of the Tenakh which contain the mitzvot

Mishnah - a collection of Jewish oral teachings

Talmud – a collection of Jewish laws that have developed over time

In the Misnah, one rabbi says, "This world is like a lobby before the Olam Ha Ba. Prepare yourself in the lobby so that you may enter the banquet hall." Similarly, the Talmud says, "This world is like the eve of Shabbat, and the Olam Ha Ba is like Shabbat. He who prepares on the eve of Shabbat will have food to eat on Shabbat." This implies that just as you must plan and prepare for a banquet or Shabbat, there must be some forethought and preparation for Olam Ha Ba as well. This could be through studying the Torah, worshipping at the synagogue or simply good deeds.

The Talmud states that all Israel has a share in the Olam Ha Ba. However, not all 'shares' are equal. A particularly righteous person will have a greater share in the Olam Ha Ba than the average person. In addition, a person can lose his share through wicked actions. This teaching could motivate Jews to follow the mitzvot carefully and build a positive relationship with God.

There are many statements in the Talmud that a particular mitzvah will guarantee a person a place in the Olam Ha Ba, or that a particular sin will lose a person's share in the Olam Ha-Ba. However, these are generally regarded as hyperbole – effectively exaggerating approval or disapproval to make a point.

The Mishnah also discusses Olam Ha Ba as a time when the dead will be resurrected. However, the focus of the discussion is about who will be resurrected rather than it being a generalised act. For example, it is said that those killed in the time of Noah's flood and in the destruction of Sodom will not be resurrected or have a place in Olam Ha Ba. This supports the idea that Olam Ha Ba will be a time in which there will be Divine justice but it's not clear whether this refers to resurrection to the afterlife, or at a time on this earth when the Messiah has arrived.

The rabbis in the Mishnah do describe Olam Ha Ba as a good thing though, for example, a single grape is said to be enough to make a whole barrel of wine. But equally, one rabbi also said that 'women will bear children daily' - which does not sound as nice!

Summary: Olam Ha Ba

- Olam Ha-Ba means the 'world to come' however there is a mixture of beliefs in Judaism as to what it is.
- Some Jews would mean a physical existence after death, whereas some believe that it is just spiritual.
- Others believe that there is no life beyond this one and Olam Ha-Ba –simply refers to the future coming of the Messiah.
- Those who do believe in the afterlife, believe that the very righteous will go to Gan Eden – a paradise.
- Whereas the average person descends to a place of punishment and/or purification, generally referred to as Gehinnom but sometimes as She'ol or by other names.
- Others say there is no literal paradise or hell, instead the righteous experience nearness to God and whatever is good in this life will be better in the world to come – one grape will make a whole flagon of wine.

10 LIVING ACCORDING TO THE TORAH

The first five books of the Jewish holy book – the Tenakh – is the Torah. These are the five books of Moses known in English as Genesis, Exodus, Leviticus, Numbers, and Deuteronomy. Jews believe that God dictated the Torah to Moses on Mount Sinai, 50 days after their exodus from Egyptian slavery.

These scared texts are written on a scroll and kept in a synagogue. The Torah is divided into 54 weekly 'portions' which are read each week at the Shabbat service. This sequence begins from the end of Sukkot – around Autumn time.

The scroll itself is handwritten in Hebrew on a parchment made from animal skin by a trained specialist called a 'sofer.' The scrolls are not directly touched when they are rolled out, but a pointer called a 'yad' is used instead. It can take up to 18 months to complete the whole process from preparing the animal skins to writing the final words. If they make any mistakes, the whole scroll becomes invalid. The finished scrolls are considered to be scared and if one is accidentally dropped in the synagogue, the whole congregation must fast for 40 days. To purposefully destroy or damage a Torah scroll is a form of antisemitism and there are countless accounts of how Jews have gone to great efforts to preserve these scrolls in times of persecution.

The Torah's stories help to share Jewish culture, and chronicle God's creation of the world followed by the establishment of Judaism through the covenants. However, the word 'Torah' can also be taken to mean the whole body of Jewish law and teaching – including the 613 mitzvot that cover all aspects of life.

The Shema

One way in which Jews observe the Torah in their day to day lives is through observing the Shema.

Deuteronomy 6 v 4-9

4   "Israel, remember this! The Lord – and the Lord alone – is our God.

5   Love the Lord your God with all your heart, with all your soul, and with all your strength.

6   Never forget these commands that I am giving you today.

7   Teach them to your children. Repeat them when
    you are at home and when you are away, when
    you are resting and when you are working.
8   Tie them on your arms and wear them on your
    foreheads as a reminder.
9   Write them on the door-posts of your houses and
    on your gates.

The first verse of the Shema, epitomises the most important belief
in Judaism – that there is only one God. The passage that follows
details how faith in God should look in practice: love God with all
that you have, teach this to your children, recite it when you wake
and before you go to sleep, and bind it to both your arm and
forehead.

As a result, the Shema is recited as a prayer daily – both morning
and night. It is declared as part of the final prayer of Yom Kippur
(the holiest day of the year), and traditionally as the last words
before death.

Jewish men use **'tefillin'** boxes whilst praying which contain
parchment with the words of Shema; these are bound to the
forehead and arm. Jewish people will also attach **'mezuzah'** to the
doorframes of their houses – which are small oblong shaped
boxes that contain the words of the Shema as well. It is a solid
reminder to everyone who enters and leaves the house that the
people living in this house are Jewish and are likely to uphold the
principles of the Shema.

Kashrut laws

The term **'kosher'** means 'fitting' or 'correct'. The word is usually used to describe foods that are made in accordance with Jewish law and allowed to be eaten. This leads to the term **kashrut,** which is the body of Jewish laws that deals with foods that Jews can and cannot eat and how these foods must be prepared and eaten. The laws of kashrut are found mainly in Leviticus 11 and Deuteronomy 14; they were among the mitzvoth given to the Jews during the period of wandering in the desert.

However, the term 'kosher' may also be used for religious objects. For example, for a **mezuzah** to be kosher, it must be written by a trained scribe on parchment. This parchment must be made from the skin of a kosher animal. Once finished carefully writing, the scribe will give it to another scribe to check. A mezuzah with mistakes or printed on paper to look like parchment is not kosher.

Food that is not kosher is known as **trefah (torn).** All plants are kosher, but not all birds, animals or fish. For an animal to be kosher it must have cloven hooves and must chew the cud. Cud is the name given to the little balls of grass that certain animals form in their stomachs after swallowing it. Later they bring up the grass into their mouths and chew it a second time before digesting it. Cows, sheep, goats and deer have these features and are therefore kosher. Pigs are not kosher, since although they have split feet they do not chew the cud. Birds are kosher if they are not birds of prey. Kosher fish can be recognized by two features. They must have fins and scales. This means that seafood is forbidden since, for example, eels do not have scales and lobsters or prawns do not have fins or scales.

Kosher animals must be killed according to the method of **shechitah.** This is a cut across the throat with a razor-sharp knife. On either side of the animal's neck are arteries that take blood to the brain. The bleeding is profuse, but the animal does not bleed to death, as is sometimes objected. The severed arteries cut off the blood supply to the brain and the animal loses consciousness immediately. Causing pain to any living animal is strictly forbidden in Jewish law. Any animal or bird that is killed by another method is not kosher. Carrying out shechitah requires a great deal of training and is a very responsible job. The person has to be deeply religious and has to have passed an examination on shechitah.

The Torah instructs Jews as to the further prohibitions that are required to satisfy the laws of kashrut. One general rule is that eating any blood from an animal or bird is forbidden. **Deuteronomy 12:23** sums up the point *'the blood is the life.'* It is therefore too sacred to be eaten. To ensure that this is achieved, once meat is purchased from the kosher butcher they are then koshered. This involves soaking the meat in water, leaving it to drain, covering the meat in salt and then rinsing again to ensure the removal of any blood. Although this procedure used to be carried out at home, today it is usually done by the butcher before the meat is sold. Even an egg may have blood in it, and once a blood spot is identified, the egg is deemed not kosher and is thrown away.

Even if the butcher does remove the blood, the observance of Kashrut makes heavy demands on the person in the kitchen, as there are special rules that must be followed here. Based on the commandment 'You must not cook a young goat in its mother's milk', **Jews who keep kosher homes do not eat meat and dairy foods together.** Meat and cheese would therefore not be cooked or served together. After a meat meal no milk products are eaten for a period of three to six hours. Meat foods may however be eaten shortly after milk foods. This separation includes not only the foods themselves, but the kitchen utensils, crockery, cutlery, washing-up bowls, dishcloths and tea towels! Every kosher kitchen is equipped with two sets of dishes: one for the meat, and one for the milk. Many Orthodox houses would have separate sinks and would colour-code utensils used for the meat in red and dairy in blue.

Foods that contain neither meat nor dairy produce are known as

parev. These foods may be eaten with either meat or dairy foods. As kashrut forbids the eating of dairy foods immediately after a meat dish many desserts have to be parev.

Following the Torah today

The Torah plays a big part in the lives of Jews today as it is believed to be the word of God. All Jews use the Torah to help guide them in their lives, but some Jews use the Torah more strictly than others. For example, some Orthodox Jews believe that it is important to follow every single rule in the Torah. However, Reform Jews tend to follow the rules they feel are most important and disregard some rules they see as outdated.

At first glance some commandments do not seem intended for the modern context. For example, in the UK we do not regularly have to literally light fires to cook or keep warm. This has therefore been interpreted by Orthodox Jews to mean they should not use an oven or switch on a light switch, but many Reform Jews say that these actions cannot be considered 'work' and that it's more work not to use them.

There are other commandments that also seem inappropriate alongside contemporary secular values. For example, there are very different views about the roles of men and women. As a result, many Reform Jews have chosen to interpret these differently or to even set these rules aside – allowing women to become Rabbis and to have a leadership role in the synagogue.

Faithfulness to the Torah has marked Jewish people out as different throughout the ages. In many ways, this has made them more vulnerable to prejudice and discrimination in society, and at its worst, persecution and genocide. However, the Jewish people also have faith that the Torah was given by God who is all-knowing and all-good; Jews can be confident that God gave them the best possible way to live, and that He wouldn't ask them to do more than is possible. Living according to the Torah ensures that the Jewish people are keeping their covenant agreement with God, and is a way to honour His faithfulness to them.

The Torah has also helped to bind the Jewish people together a community – from a family level to a global scale. Reliving the stories of the past, and knowing that the same rules have been followed for centuries, helps them to feel a deep connection with their ancestors and those who will come after them.

The Torah ensures that justice is upheld, and that people are treated equally. Many of the laws are the foundation of the UK's own legal system. It is said that by keeping to this higher standard of morality, the Jews are able to be 'a light to the nations' - showing what people can be. For many, by keeping to the Torah, it is hoped that the world will simply become a better place.

Summary: Living According to the Torah

- The Torah is God's law which is found in the Hebrew Bible.
- It contains 613 laws which relate to all aspects of life.
- The Torah is what gives Jewish people their unique identity.
- The Torah is the focal point of worship and is given special treatment in the synagogue.
- The Torah contains the covenant God has made with the Jewish people to be his Chosen People

- The scriptures will tell Jewish people the rituals that they have to carry out daily – food laws etc.
- The scriptures can inform the Jewish people about what they are to believe in.
- It can give Jewish people moral guidance in helping them to live a good life – it gives them direction.
- It helps them with their prayer life and how to worship properly.
- It gives them a sense of history and belonging as they see the history of the Jewish people.

Orthodox
- Orthodox Jews very strict. They take a literal view of the Torah.
- They believe that God revealed all the instructions they need to know for life.
- These are the 613 mitzvoth contained in the Torah.
- These rules must be carefully interpreted and obeyed.
- Interpretations of the laws are contained in Talmud. The rituals of worship, the celebration of festivals and the rules for everyday living remain the same throughout history.
- Wrong to allow historical events and social changes to influence the interpretation of God's word.

Reform
- Do not believe that the Torah is the exact word of God and so it is not considered as a divine code of conduct.
- God wants the rules to be kept but they must be applied to a modern context.
- Stress the historical basis for Judaism and so are happy to make changes to rituals such as synagogue worship as long as the essence is kept.
- The Hebrew language is difficult to read and understand. It should be translated into the languages of the people, this means it needs to change.

11 WORSHIP

Whilst worship is a commandment found in the Torah, ultimately it is an act of love for God which strengthens an individual's relationship with Him. It is an opportunity to thank Him for things that He has done, and it is an important part of the Covenantal agreement with God.

However, as much of Jewish worship is communal, it also helps to strengthen the Jewish Community whilst often bringing both spiritual and physical refreshment.

Worship can take place in either the synagogue or the home. Often, there is actually more emphasis on worship at home – for example, the Sedar meal is the focus of Pesach, and much of Shabbat is observed at home.

Worshipping in the synagogue

Orthodox synagogues hold three daily services in Hebrew. The services include: shacharit (early morning), minchah (afternoon) and ma'ariv (evening).

Men and women sit separately, and men cover their heads with a kippah, which is a skull cap. Some very observant Jewish men were a kippah or other head covering all the time.

Observant men usually go to the synagogue as there is an obligation to pray with a minyan (group of 10 men or more gathered for prayer and worship). Women are not under any obligation to pray but can choose to do so.

The tallit or prayer shawl is worn every day for morning prayers by Orthodox men. They will also wear tefillin. The tallit is a long fringed shawl (usually white) with blue or black stripes. The fringes make eight strands and five knots at each corner. These fringes are called tzizit and in the Hebrew numbering system the letters of tzizit are equal to 600.

600 + 8 (strands) + 5 (knots) = 613 (mitzvoth)

There are no particular dress requirements for women other than to dress modestly. Some orthodox women wear a head covering (or wig) called a sheitel.

Reform synagogues don't have daily services like those held in Orthodox synagogues, but they do have a service on Shabbat. The services are in both Hebrew and the language of the country the synagogue is in. Men and women sit together and often musical instruments are played.

The service

Services are usually led by a rabbi but anyone with religious knowledge can lead worship. For Orthodox Jews the rabbi must be a man, but Reform Jewish rabbis can be women.

All synagogues have a large cupboard facing Jerusalem called the aron hakodesh, which symbolises the Ark of the Covenant that held the tablets of stone with the Ten Commandments received by Moses. It is the centrepiece of the synagogue and holds the Torah scrolls. Often a cantor, called the hazzan, stands at the front facing the aron hakodesh to lead prayers, which are often sung or chanted.

A prayer book containing the three daily prayers called the **siddur** is used during each service. The opening prayers are usually said, followed by a recitation of the Shema.

'Hear O Israel! The Lord is our God, the Lord is One.'

The Amidah is a prayer that is central to Jewish worship. It is performed standing and in silence while facing Jerusalem. Worshippers think over the words in their minds rather than saying them out loud.

The Amidah prayer consists of blessings split into three sections:

- Praising God and asking for His mercy
- Asking God for help
- Thanking God

Services also contain readings from the Torah. These are followed by final prayers, such as the Aleinu, which is a prayer to praise God.

Summary: worship

- Jewish worship takes place at the synagogue and in the home.
- Orthodox synagogues hold three daily prayer services.
- Orthodox men and women sit separately in the synagogue.
- Worship is one of the 613 mitzvot.
- Jewish men pray as a group of ten men called a minyan.
- A tallit (prayer shawl) is worn by Jewish men to pray.
- Services in the synagogue are usually led by the Rabbi.
- Worship in the synagogue is a key aspect of the High holiday Rosh Hashanah and Yom Kippur.

Printed in Great Britain
by Amazon

27184373R00046